Written by Corinne Courtalon
Illustrated by Christian Broutin

Specialist Adviser:
Jean Vercoutter
Member of the French Academy
of Inscriptions and Fine Arts

ISBN 0-944589-07-3
First U.S. Publication 1988 by
Young Discovery Library
217 Main St. • Ossining, NY 10562

©1986 by Editions Gallimard
Translated by Sarah Matthews
English text © 1988 by Moonlight Publishing Ltd.
Thanks to Tom O'Connell

YOUNG DISCOVERY LIBRARY

On the Banks
of the
Pharaoh's Nile

Evan Coyne

YOUNG DISCOVERY LIBRARY

Over three thousand years ago, there lived in Egypt a peaceful, learned people. They loved building beautiful houses, and magnificent temples and palaces. Over the centuries, desert sand has blown over and into their buildings, burying them and hiding them from sight.
How can we find out how the Ancient Egyptians lived? By patiently clearing away the sand.

This is what archaeologists do to find statues, furniture, pottery, paintings, and even golden treasure, all left behind by the Ancient Egyptians. Special archaeologists called Egyptologists study the finds to learn all they can about the way of life in Egypt at that time.

If you go to museums like the Field Museum in Chicago, or the Metropolitan in New York, you will see some of the Ancient Egyptian objects which have been rescued from the sand.

It is very hot in Egypt. Most of the country is sandy desert, where rain hardly ever falls, nothing can grow, and no one can live.

Desert animals: scarab beetle, scorpion, vulture; gazelle, lion and viper. A scorpion sting can kill a small child.

Egypt is in Northeast Africa.

The Nile valley is shown in green.

But there is a huge river, the Nile, which flows through the desert for 4,000 miles. The Ancient Egyptians live along the riverbank. The river gives them water, and makes the ground damp for crops. In the summer, the sun becomes so hot it seems everything will burn up. But then the Nile swells with water and overflows its banks into the valley. Three months later, it goes down.

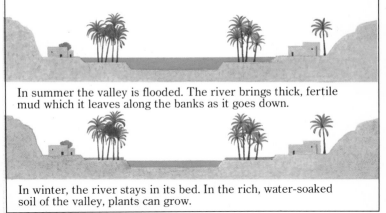

In summer the valley is flooded. The river brings thick, fertile mud which it leaves along the banks as it goes down.

In winter, the river stays in its bed. In the rich, water-soaked soil of the valley, plants can grow.

Boats travel up and down the Nile: boats with sails, boats with oars carrying goods, and little ferryboats flitting from one side of the river to the other. Fishermen make themselves very light small boats from the papyrus reeds which grow along the riverbank. The pharaoh and his court travel in beautiful painted boats with rows and rows of oars.

Hunters kill ducks and geese with throwing sticks a little like boomerangs.

The river is teeming with fish:
eels, carp, catfish, tench. The Egyptians
make a sort of caviar from
mullet eggs. But there are crocodiles
in the river too, and hippopotami. They
can sometimes tip over a boat and
sink it. Noblemen enjoy going out on
hippopotamus hunts with ropes and
harpoons. And on the riverbank there
are cobras — their bite can kill!

The crown of the
Northern Kingdom

The crown of the
Southern Kingdom

The crown of Egypt

The pharaoh is a very powerful king. The Egyptians believe that he is the son of the sun, and that he has supernatural powers. They call him God-King. What does he look like? Around the temples are huge statues of the pharaohs, like the one in the picture on the left. Often he wears a headcloth over his wig: the nemes. On his chin he has a false beard, and on his forehead the uraeus. This is a little golden cobra which protects the king.

The pharaoh wears a kepresh on his head.

The queen

The prince is holding a lotus flower.

There are crowds of servants to wait on the pharaoh.

Friendly nations bring expensive presents for him.

He orders palaces, tombs and temples to be built.

The pharaoh likes to go lion hunting in his chariot.

Egypt is a rich land, and Egyptians are content to stay within its borders. But then they move further afield, becoming known as top **warriors.**

Prisoners

Under the pharaohs they conquer a great empire, from Syria to the Sudan. The army is huge and well trained. **Prisoners of war** are used as servants, or in gold mines or stone quarries.

As wars go on, the Egyptians begin to lose — first to the powerful Nubians and then the Persians. Later the Greeks, then the Romans, cross the sea to do battle. In time, the mighty Egyptians are overrun. And sand will cover the temples.

The Egyptians write in hieroglyphics.

Scribes help the pharaoh.

They are very important, because they can read and write. They are sent all over Egypt to keep watch over the harvests and the building of the temples. Occasionally they make expeditions into the desert to bring back precious metals and jewels.

How can you become a scribe?

By learning to read, write and count. You start on clay tablets, then, when you are good enough, you can write with pen and ink on a fine roll of **papyrus,** or paper. Because it rolls up it is easy to carry around and store.

Papyrus is a plant which grows near the Nile. The stalk is trimmed, then stripped and flattened to make paper.

After the floods, the fields are sown. Cattle are
led over the fields to tread the seeds deep into the mud.

**The fields need water
from the Nile to grow crops.**
The farmers use a 'shadoof.'
It's a pole with a bucket on
one end and a weight on the
other end. The pole swings
around from the river and
tips water into the **irrigation
canals.** Harvests are rich
in Egypt. On the next page
you see a scribe. He watches
the harvest and notes the size
of the crop.

Hoe

Carpenter's tool

Knife   Awl

The Egyptians wear a lot of makeup. They put black kohl all around their eyes to protect them from the glare of the sun.

They love going up on to the flat roofs of their houses to chat in the cool of the evening.

What do the Egyptians wear?

The men wear a linen skirt, the women a long linen dress, while the children often don't wear anything at all. Rich Egyptians wear heavy wigs to show how important they are. The women's wigs are longer than the men's and have turquoise or gold beads braided into the ends.

What are their houses like?

They are built of mud bricks, then painted in bright colors. They have flat roofs, often with silos on them to store the grain. In the gardens, papyrus and sycamores grow around a pool.

The Egyptians love cats. They train them to go hunting. A lot of cats are even mummified after they die.

Mirror

Makeup spoon

Bracelet

Sandals

Look at these household objects.
They're not very different from ours...

Egyptians eat their meals sitting around a low table. They sit on the ground or on low stools. They drink beer out of cups, and don't use plates. Everyone just picks what they want out of the dish with their fingers. What do they eat? Mostly fish, onions and bread, but also birds, beef, lettuce, lentils, cucumbers, dates...The Egyptians make things out of wood: chairs, tables, and wooden headrests which they use as pillows. The rich have ornate beds with carved legs. They have beautiful jewelry made from gold and precious stones.

Skimmers

Sieve

Broom

Chair

Headrest

Bed

The Egyptians love family life.
They particularly like playing games
together: dice, knuckle-bones,
checkers, and a game like
Parchesi called 'senet'.
**The very rich arrange splendid
feasts for their friends.** On their
heads they wear cones of scented
grease which melt and drip down
their faces, cooling them pleasantly as
the party wears on! There is an
orchestra, and dancers to amuse the
guests. The musicians play the harp,
the lute, and the flute. The dancers
beat time with small rattles called
'sistra'.

Children's toys: a leopard with a mouth that
opens, a pull-along horse on wheels, a doll.

**Boys and girls prefer more active
games:** shooting arrows at targets,
wrestling, or a game rather like our
piggy-back. Little children have
lovely toys made out of wood and
fabric: spinning tops, balls, dolls, and
animals on wheels to pull along.

A ball game

Ra Isis Osiris Horus Anubis Hathor

Who are all these people with animal heads or strange crowns?

They are the gods who watch over the Egyptians. They each have their own great temples. Nobody is allowed in except the priests. Each god has his own statue deep in the most secret room of his temple. Sometimes, on feast days, the statues of the gods are carried out and the priests and people walk with them in long processions.

The two enormous stone needles standing at the front of the temple are called obelisks.

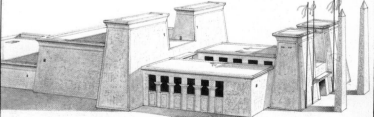

Have you heard of the Pyramids of Egypt? They stand in the desert, safely away from the Nile floods. They are gigantic tombs. Inside each pyramid is a maze of secret galleries leading to the room where the pharaoh's mummy in its coffin lies hidden.

Pyramid of Cheops:
1. Chamber of the King
2. Treasure room
3. An unfinished chamber
4. Great gallery
5. Air shaft

The Pyramids of Cheops,
Khephren and Mykerinus.
A causeway links them to
the Temple of the Valley,
from where a canal goes to the Nile.

Next to the burial chamber are rooms
filled with furniture, vases and
precious things: **the pharaoh's
treasures.** The pyramid has been
designed so that it's almost
impossible to get inside once the
pharaoh has been buried. The
entrance is hidden and the
galleries leading to the king's
burial chamber are
blocked off to stop
graverobbers.
The tallest Egyptian
pyramid of all is the tomb
of Cheops: it measures
480 feet in height.

It can take over thirty years to build a pyramid. First the stone has to be brought in. Some stones are close by in the desert, but others, like granite, have to come from quarries far away. The stone has to be loaded onto boats and floated down the Nile. Then the stones are dragged on rollers to the place where the pyramid is to be built.

Some of the blocks of stone weigh over twenty tons, and without having any cranes it seems impossible to get them up to build the pyramid walls. So the Egyptians make huge ramps of brick all around the pyramid. Then the stone can be hauled right up to the top. The pharaoh makes the peasants do this sort of work. The pyramids rose up into the sky, showing the greatness of the dead pharaoh — and of the living Egypt.

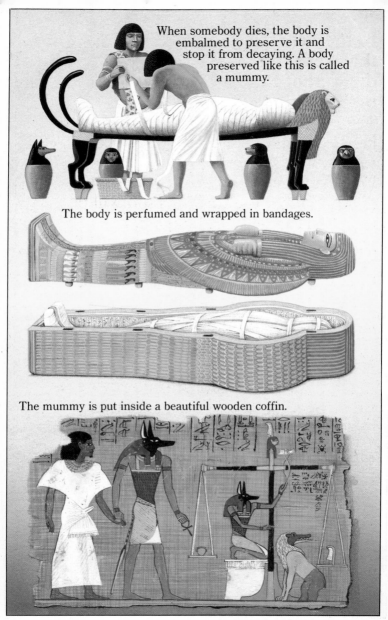

When somebody dies, the body is embalmed to preserve it and stop it from decaying. A body preserved like this is called a mummy.

The body is perfumed and wrapped in bandages.

The mummy is put inside a beautiful wooden coffin.

In the desert, there are tombs dug out of the mountainsides. They are like real houses, with lots of rooms. The Ancient Egyptians believe there is a life after death. So that the dead person will be happy in the land of the dead, the walls are painted with pictures of the Nile, and of the animals and people living along its banks. The rooms are filled with beautiful furniture and 'shabtis' are put all around the mummy. What are shabtis? They are little statues of servants for the dead person. The most thoughtful provide three hundred and sixty-five shabtis — one for each day of the year!

◄ The dead live in another world, protected by the god Anubis and ruled over by Osiris.

To get to the desert, where the dead are buried, the bodies have to be carried across the Nile.

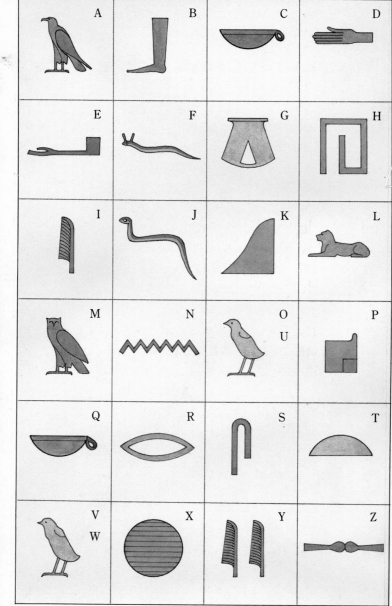

Writing with pictures.

Egyptian writing was done with little drawings — of plants, animals or signs. Put together these drawings are called **hieroglyphics.** Archaeologists found these drawings carved on the walls of temples and on statues. Others were on papyrus or painted on walls of tombs.

What do they mean?

For almost 2,000 years it was a mystery. One day a stone was found, with three kinds of writing on it. One was hieroglyphics. By comparing the words with the drawings we learned what they meant. The mystery was over! Each drawing was a letter!

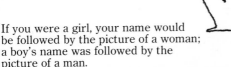

If you were a girl, your name would be followed by the picture of a woman; a boy's name was followed by the picture of a man.

Thus Horus, son of Isis,
Saith to divine Osiris,
"O Father, I have brought to thee
This vindicated spirit.

"His deeds have been adjudged,
His heart weighed in the Balance;
Grant him thy cakes and ale, and grant
Him welcome in thy presence."

From the Book of the Dead
About 3,500 B.C.

Index